BEYOND GESTURES

BEYOND GESTURES

Gabriel and Marcel Piqueray

translated by
Robert Archambeau & Jean-Luc Garneau

MADHAT PRESS
CHESHIRE, MASSACHUSETTS

MadHat Press
MadHat Incorporated
PO Box 422, Cheshire, MA 01225

Copyright © 2024 by MadHat Press
Copyright © 2024 Translators, Robert Archambeau & Jean-Luc Garneau
All rights reserved.

Belgian copyright: *Au-delà des gestes et autre textes*
© 1993 Éditions Labor

Introduction by Robert Archambeau

The Library of Congress has assigned
this edition a Control Number of
2024948845

ISBN 978-1-952335-89-1 (paperback)

Words by Gabriel and Marcel Piqueray
Cover image: *Twins in Big Shoes* (2024) by Sophia Santos
Cover design by Marc Vincenz

www.MadHat-Press.com

First Printing
Printed in the United States of America

Table of Contents

Introduction: A Piqueray Dossier *by Robert Archambeau* ... ix

Beyond Gestures

The Raft Of The Medusa	3
Hidden Light	4
Heavy Dust	5
Miracle of the Wolves	6
The Affective Distance Game	8
Hierarchy: A Night	10
Beauty In Season	11
Artists	12
Mystery's Sorcery	13
Pantomime	14
A Day in the Life of Mésange	15
What Happens in a Golden Summer	16
The Archdukes	17
The Flagellant	18
Hostages	19
The Woman from Alsace	20
Riding At Night	21
Everyday Life	22
The Scream	23
Delirium's Kingdom	24
Sideshows of the Sky	25
The Great Terror	26

The Lovely Little Bath

The Five-Cent Ultrasound	29
The Moratorium	30
Darling Potatoes	31

Clitarabelles

Clitarabelles	35
White Ducklings	36

Uninhibited Poems

Male and Female Cousins, with Technician
   Note
   Urgent Poem   42
   Comfortable Poem   43
   Poem Ending a Task   44
   Poem à la Papa   45
   Poem or Not   46
Proceleusmatics and Amphibraques
   Preface: Strup Stroup   47
   Gas Bubbles   49
   May They Survive Raging Tarragon   50
   However a Note in The Margin   51
   If Dirty Cart-Greased to the Gaiters   52
   A Pedal-Pusher Said to Me   53
Baby Clothes
   To the Reader   55
   Envoi   56
   The Sranza de Lustuk-Obritch   57
   Note   58
   Bulgaria, My Country   59
High Eggs
   Foreword   60
   Calle-Grattoir   61
   Calle-Grattoir 2   62
   Fous-La Lente   63
   Prose-Site   64
   Tout Chez (Touché)   65
Uninhibited Poems
   Pubis of Mite   67
The Sproks
   Preface   69
   Tale of an Experiment   70
   Example of an Activity   71

An Action Among Others	72
Tale of Another Action	73
An Activity Among Others	74

Die Damen

Private Life	79
Young Rays	80
Die Damen	81

Tobacco Monument

Look at Louze	89
Laura	90
Flowing Water	91
The Hungarian	92
Professionals	93
Light	94

Unpublished Writings

The Lover	99
Heart Phosphor	100
The Sealed Mountain	102
Uncertainty in Love	103
For My Fiancée	104
Gudrun	106

About the Authors	107

Introduction: A Piqueray Dossier

Gabriel and Marcel Piqueray were identical twins, born in Brussels in 1920. Surrealists, they associated with key figures of the movement, including André Breton and René Magritte (with whom they held regular "surrealist working meetings" for many years), as well as with the musician Chet Baker and the composer Francis Poulenc. In 1957 they became joint editors of the influential avant-garde journal *Phantomas*, whose contributors included Samuel Beckett, Roland Barthes, René Magritte, Kurt Schwitters, and Jorge Luis Borges, among many others. They published a dozen books together, always listing "Gabriel and Marcel Piqueray" as authors— the Piqueray brothers did not believe in individual authorship. They also co-authored with Paul Colinet. Gabriel Piqueray died in 1992, Marcel in 1997. Recordings of their work were released on the Sub Rosa label in the collection *Le Groupe Surrealiste Revolutionnaire*.

The scholar Michel Delville gives some idea of their context:

> *Correspondance*, the first Belgian Surrealist magazine, was founded by Paul Nougé, Camille Goemans and Marcel Lecomte in 1924, the same year as Breton's first manifesto. Since that time, Belgian poetry has remained one the European avant-garde's best-kept secrets. The names of Nougé, Chavée and Dumont are conspicuously absent from most anthologies and literary histories, and Belgian surrealism is generally considered as a non-literary phenomenon and almost systematically confined to the paintings of René Magritte and Paul Delvaux. Unlike many other Belgian writers who moved to Paris to make a career (the examples of Georges Simenon, Henri Michaux, Pierre Alechinsky and many others come to mind) most Belgian surrealists published their work in their home country, and this may explain their lack of recognition outside a small circle of connoisseurs and specialists. Perhaps it is the sense of being relegated to the margins of francophone culture that accounts, at least in part, for the radical, convulsive spirit that runs through the history of the Belgian counterculture.

Critic Philippe Dewolf describes the nature of the Piquerays' joint authorship and collective sensibility:

> It has been noted that their sensibilities and their characters are essentially different. On occasion, of course, a few words or lines by one of them appear in the other's text, but not often. Usually, only the signature is in common. As Marcel Piqueray explained in 1944, their names had been and would remain inseparable: 'one signature, one station signal, as they say on radio; one overall station signal for the Piquerist state of mind.' Five concerns characterize this Piquarist state of mind: the quotidian, angst, tenderness, the fantastic, and humor.

If the two Piqueray twins are one, they are also many. Much of the Piquerays' work that appeared in *Phantomas* involved a kind of Pessoa-like creation of different poetic personae, and it is here where their absurdism and oddball humor come into play. In this collection, the persona poetry, along with spurious notes about the putative authors, is included in the "Uninhibited Poems" section. Some of this work is scatological, some straight-up goofy. This, I'm sure, is what an anonymous reference book writer had in mind when he wrote:

> If there is a quality specific to Franco-Belgian literature, it is a corrosive humor raised to its highest point by the surrealists. It is also the attribute of *Phantomas*, a literary and pictorial review emphasizing the ludic and enlivened by the "*Sept types en or*" (Seven Golden Guys): Paul Bourgoignie, François Jacqmin, Joseph Noiret, Pierre Puttemans, Theodore Koenig, and Marcel and Gabriel Piqueray. *Phantomas* is perhaps the best illustration of this *Belgique sauvage*, which contrasts a little too easily with the official Belgium.

"The Sproks," one persona-based series included in the present collection, is a manifestation of the humorous side of the Piqueray twins. The series has a kind of strange, Buster Keaton-style slapstick, combined with a satire of bourgeois propriety, and even a satire of scientific method. Michel Delville has this to say about "The Sproks":

Beyond Gestures

To me, the "Sproks" poems have always resembled a cross between Satie, Beckett, Buñuel, and Laurel and Hardy. The proximity of food, garbage and shit in the poetry of the Piqueray Brothers points to a poetics that does not shy away from describing fantasies of infantile regression and puts them to the service of a popular art that delights in imagining how the most banal situations can degenerate into absurdist extremes. Such manifestations of the eccentric, the repellent and the abject create a space where the shock aesthetics of the revolutionary avant-garde meets the verbal games of the poète-farceur, who considers poetry as a form of linguistic slapstick comedy. For all its apparent timelessness and impersonality, the poetry of the Piqueray Brothers remains rooted in their cultural and social background, and one suspects that many of the "Non-Inhibited Poems" were inspired by the chink of beer bottles, the smell of fried sausages and the sight of people pissing in the streets on their way back from the local café. As Louis Scutenaire once put it, in Belgium:

> *On boit de la bière et on mange de la viande*
> *Et tout le monde est une bande d'abrutis*

> We drink beer and we eat meat
> And we're all just a bunch of morons.

Long live *la Belgique sauvage!* Long live beer and slapstick! Long live *les frères* Piqueray! I hope you enjoy their company as much as I do.

—Robert Archambeau

Beyond Gestures

*for Marcel Lecomte
the erased spectator*

The Raft Of The Medusa

for Geneviève, for Nathalie, for Jacques

I speak of the folding, Y-shaped cane, a tool often used by hunters and horse-racing regulars—the former to make their aim more deadly, the latter as a portable, revolving chair, to follow more easily the movements of their circling horses.

They say that Formality, everywhere, uses his all the time, being so stunned and so breathless at the merest suggestion of the chanciness of life.

Hidden Light

This stately, low-wheeled carriage loaded with bright yellow boards never ceases to amaze people when they see it coming around the corner of the deserted street, pushed by a man in an apron.

It is such a strange vehicle, too majestic for this kind of cargo, such an unexpected and improvised means of transport—but somehow you know you've seen it before, though you can't remember where. You're so sure of this that you're fixated by the sight of it, trivial as can be, as it rolls silently down the middle of the quiet street, through the middle of neighborhoods of accumulated memories through which we must walk, to understand.

Heavy Dust

for Ann, to ***, for Paul Colinet and (in principle)
for everyone in the Universe who, etc. etc.

In the forest of chairs the spotlights hunt the shadows. Having found them, they coil there, gathering their courage. They wait and watch, greedily taking in the secrets that, even now, they spy in the large armchairs upholstered with shimmering light.

The feet of the chairs, their backs, their arms all eye each other, crouching in waiting, ready to ambush one another. Roving battles rage, velvet against velvet.

Surrounded in the heart of the forest of chairs, the beds rally. Arching up, rearing high, their coiled springs suddenly freeze, and they stumble, seized up in the tremendous heat.

Beams of light seize on the cushions with an unheard-of violence, then catch the great table and the low doors. The forest gives off a thick smoke-stench as the light burns it away.

Now constellations of dust particles whirl in the great volumes of light.

In the forest of chairs, nothing is left but this glimmering load of heavy dust, falling like ruin on a forest silent with fear, a naked forest playing at death.

The reign of chiaroscuro has come.

Miracle of the Wolves

"All the roads to Angoulême are closed!" shouted Bolar, crouching at the edge of the ditch, a black shawl twisted over his thick hair.

Immense clouds soared across the sky. The clouds roiled ferociously as the wind's roar grew and grew. Noble and erect, the trees pushed high into the sky, their limbs swinging left and right in grand and regal gestures. Torn branches crashed into the bushes, bouncing wildly.

Suddenly, a group of people appeared in the distance: they too were walking toward Angoulême.

"They won't get through!" Bolar roared, "They won't get through! The roads are blocked!... The roads are blocked!..." He rose anxiously.

The little troop grew nearer. Bolar thought they must be beggars or, even better, a gang of outcasts and perverts. But soon he was able to make out the features of the new arrivals: lion-headed knights, chimney sweeps sporting red gladioli, gypsies masked with green laurels.

An old man wearing a cone of wicker for a hat broke from their ranks, his stride thrown off by a club foot, and drawing up next to Bolar whispered into his ear, saying: "You had a dream last night, I know it. Don't deny it, don't lie to me. It was heresy. You were cycling down the main street of your town, when a black basset hound charged up behind you and caught you by the heel. Then you got off your bike, threw yourself onto someone's front steps and pushed the howling thing away with your elbows. Don't worry, all this will come out. Godless acts and dreams do not go unpunished. Someday, maybe four or five hundred years from now, some learned person will write all your crimes down in a book."

And the old man danced away to his masked band, with its wild and alien gestures.

Just then a sound like the shattering of immense windows came down from high above. Craning their necks, everyone looked up and saw, high above, something huge and made, it seemed, of a pale, yellowish wood. It was an enormous necklace. "The Sign!" they yelled, "The Sign!" And they threw themselves down into the dust of the road, shivering and brimming over with fear.

The necklace came down slowly through the vastness of the sky. Bolar, eyes glued to this wonder, stepped over the prostrate bodies of the dancers, and, straddling the ditch, strode toward the nearest field. There could be no doubt: it was a necklace of light oak, gigantic, in which were set brilliant diamonds the size of apples. It soon dominated the landscape.

Just then Bolar became a wolf.

That evening, the same road lay crusted with snow under a sky full of stars, while thousands of wolves loped steadily toward Angoulême. The pealing of bells cut through the air, the signal that the roads leading to the city were now open.

And the wolves coursed on in their pack, shiny-eyed, each wearing around its neck a little necklace of light oak gleaming with precious stones.

The Affective Distance Game

"Vendôme ..." sighed the Marquise, leaning from the battlements of her turret.

"My jewel!" the Duke cried from the foot of the tower. He pulled a few ivy leaves from the wall and pressed them against his lips, tasting their bitterness. Faint voices came to them from far off in the splendid summer evening.

Some said, "Limousin! Golden Age! Rocamadour!" Others called out gently, "The Princes of the Blood! Saint-Amant-Roche-Savine! Ribérac!" Still others asked, "Blois? Marie-Adelaïde? Milady?"

"No, no, this is awful!" cried the Marquise, in answer. A great commotion was heard from up above. Then, suddenly, nothing.

Thinking this must be some kind of a joke, the Duke raised his eyes toward the turret's battlements, and took a few impatient steps toward the moat. He laughed heartily:

"Bridgit!—What's she up to? Oh, she's in for it now!"

But still silence reigned.

From the distant woods he could hear the faint sound of young ladies dancing. Then came new voices, with an echo like the omen of a terrible sorrow.

It was a group of lords, rounding the bend with a little band of armed men. They bore the corpse of a young man.

Seeing this, the Duke turned abruptly back to face the castle, its battlements now shining violently in the moonlight.

"He played the game," the armed men explained, "And fell dead the moment the Marquise sobbed out her last answer."

But the Duke was no longer listening. He had stepped lightly to one side. "Good God," he murmured, "I could have sworn they didn't love each other that much...."

Striding up to the tower, he stepped on a square of blue silk, spotted with a little blood: it was a woman's handkerchief. He quickened his pace.

Arriving at the summit of the turret, he found all the players gathered there. He went straight to the little knot of princesses. In their arms they held the corpse of the Marquise, her dead face bathed in the purest light.

Hierarchy: A Night

"Can you see anything?" shouted Danour. He raised the faint and flickering lantern to his face. His squinting features showed his worry.

"I think this road winds on down the mountain," Lora answered. "Too bad it's so dark tonight. No time to be stuck on the summit, with all this wind—it's not going to be comfortable."

Danour laughed. "To hell with comfort" he said. "The important thing is for us to get down to the valley." The words had hardly left his mouth when he stubbed his toe against a human body. It moved. A voice spoke.

"I don't want to butt in here, but let me tell you this: you'd better not try to go down there." The speaker struggled to sit up, rubbing the sleep from his eyes.

Danour brought his lantern over to have a look at this unexpected dispenser of wisdom. It was a man, about forty, with a big moustache and a bowler hat. As the man stood up he went on explaining: "You see," he said, "at first the summit was covered with lost couples and young families. The brave ones, though, were able to find their way down into the valley. The rest followed. By now they've worked out a system: every family's got its place, packed in side by side from the top on down. You and the missus here will be the final link—you can settle down right here."

"Now, he added, "let me get some sleep. I'm really tired. Good night."

Down in the valley, it sounded like someone got a foot tangled up in the strings of a harp, then became overly-apologetic, making careful and elaborate excuses.

Beauty In Season

She was a woman very proper in her bearing, her speech and, perhaps, her character. When she spoke she would arrange her hair with a sudden movement of her hand, pushing it back with the easy grace possessed by only the rarest of women. Then her hand would return, softly, to her body, to rest on her joined knees.

Her conversation was unforced, her eyes always fixed respectfully on yours. While speaking she'd let her tongue glide lightly to her lips as she pronounced certain words: *praline, humid, jewel, garden.*

Sometimes, too—for she spoke well on a wide variety of topics—sometimes, during a theoretical exposition, she would stretch out an arm, take up a book, promptly pull her skirt back into place, and read, with great poise, a seemingly trivial sentence. She would roll her r's ever so slightly: "...soon the volume of the overflow will surpass the volume of the capacity of the reservoir, and its contents will roil violently. At this point, the contracting muscles will repeatedly activate an exhaust valve, leading to a forceful expulsion …" or "… these elements, because they contain many extremely sensitive particles, play an important role in the attaining of pleasure…."

Invariably, she would hold her listener completely in her power; her terrifying, sublime, famous and inexorable spell.

In the end, she would rise and leave the room laughing, her supple, reptilian body gliding through the breezy chambers of victory and night.

Artists

for Jacques Calonne

In an immense glass hall, six hundred and twenty-five men, wearing only delicate black silk socks that sculpt their otherwise naked legs, have just mounted racing bikes with elegantly curving handle bars. The wheels are mounted on rotating steel cylinders driven by electrical motors.

Twenty-five rows of twenty-five participants fill the vast room. Each man is isolated from his immediate neighbors by a space of about twenty-five square meters, at the center of which he prepares for the performance.

In the back of the hall, facing the cyclists, an orchestra composed mainly of trumpets, flutes, fifes, and ocarinas tunes up, as is the custom before the real show begins.

At the appointed time a technician throws a switch, setting in motion the twelve hundred and fifty cylinders and, therefore, the wheels of the bicycles. At the same time, the orchestra begins playing *moderato*, a tempo barely half the speed intended for this piece. The audience, meanwhile, watches the orchestra attentively, through binoculars issued to them before the show began.

The orchestra performs with a rare consistency, and (it is worth noting) with excellent support from the fifes playing in the background.

The whole ceremony comes to an end with a passage repeated in forte, each phrase punctuated by the cyclists. Having let their pedals go, they kick (first with their ridiculously stiffened right feet, then their left), at big gold-lamé balloons hurled at their legs by a well-timed machine expertly engineered for just this purpose.

Mystery's Sorcery

The Room of Fire is of infinite volume.
    Its walls are a supple skin of cork.
    At the edge of its vastness stand slate benches on which have been placed, at regular intervals, huge chalk basins brimming with grains of lead.
    On the walls hang gold calabashes stuffed with soft chunks of bread. Long rosaries droop floorward from the ceiling, each bead the size of a man's head. The balls are made of white felt punctured by glass daggers.
    At the very heart of the Room of Fire lies the Basin of the Damned. It is enormous, and brims with a liquid the exact color of the rainbow.
    When a great silence falls over the Room of Fire, six masked women come and lie down beside the Basin of the Damned.
    They rise at the slightest sound, and dance a sacred round called the Dance of the Flames.
    As the choreographed movements go on, the women begin to glow, until they are covered with fecund, darting flames.
    Living torches, they whirl until a great silence once again fills the Room of Fire.
    They say that this room is dedicated to the Sorcery of Mystery.

Pantomime

Snaking up from the basket, the rubber hose stops level with the top of the stone bench.

There is very little open space on the bench between the seated King and Queen.

Suddenly Iris pops the door open, waving with her gloved right hand in the kind of gesture that says: "Come on, come on, I'm waiting for you."

Digitale gets up, walks over to the door that Iris has now snapped shut behind herself. Just as Digitale is about to open it, she catches the murmur of wind in the grove's distant tree tops. Pausing, she cranes her neck, looking toward the pond.

Off in the distance, bison hulk toward the train station. Instinctively, they tread the banks, avoiding the railroad tracks.

Digitale sets out along the high, wisteria-draped wall, where woolly, emerald vines droop from old rusty nails.

She savors the perfumed evening air, stopping, brow furrowed, to listen to the strange sound made by what must be something falling freely down through the open space above. She lifts her face toward the sky, taking in the essence of the moment.

Then, with an offhanded certainty, she slowly wraps her fingers around the rung nearest to her hand and, without a second thought, starts to climb the ladder that soars up from the damp sand and reaches, straight and narrow, to the sky.

A Day in the Life of Mésange

"I'm going to eat sand," announced Mésange.

Then she started working the sewing machine. The machine itself sat high on a table with propped-up legs. To reach the pedal, Mésange had to strain, lifting her leg uncomfortably high. Soon this wore her out, and she lifted first her left leg, then her right, in a tremendous effort completely disproportionate to the end result.

Things did not go well: the machine worked erratically, grinding terribly and constantly threatening to flip over and crash to the kitchen floor. Mésange kept at it, though, pushing the pedal harder and harder, sweating to make the wheel go just a little bit faster.

In the end, noticing that the object pierced by the needle was no mere handkerchief but the smooth, shiny body of a fish, she gave it up, letting her tired legs rest.

Her father, seeing her sighing and easing her her right leg down gingerly, said: "Come on Mésange, cheer up. Sure, today may not have been a big success. But so what? Don't let it get you down: tomorrow's another day! You're a resourceful girl—where's your confidence! Think of the future!"

Consoled, Mésange went and kissed her dolls, set the table, and played at cooking sand.

What Happens in a Golden Summer

The princess passes: a visit to the Hall of Mirrors. The guards are there, smoking their pipes. She takes a pipe from one of them, tastes it: it is unpleasantly bitter. There is blood on the pipe.

The princess passes: a visit to the geometric gardens. Dukes, barons, and marquises loiter by the hedges. The August evening is thick with lilac. Her breast heaves deeply as she takes in the scented air. There is blood on the lilacs.

The princess passes: a visit to the kitchens. There, she finds boards laden with roasted joints, orange peel, pheasant feathers, sage bouquets. The smell of garlic, the scent of burning evergreens, clouds of gnats. Two servants fight behind the princess. Their struggle is fierce and cunning. One of them pulls out his knife, and hurls it at his rival. The blade whirls through the air, missing its goal. The princess is hit, cries out and falls dead, the dagger in her back.

A storm bursts over all of France.

There is blood in the King's kitchens.

The Archdukes

for Jean-Clarence Lambert

It was never without some degree of apprehension that Claude, his arms laden with plates of oysters, entered the bedroom he rented from one of his friends, a grave-digger. He always knew he'd find his sister Clio in the bed, wearing nothing but a green wool sweater. This was a woman to whom the convolutions of a particularly involved inheritance case had united Claude in holy matrimony.

Most days he'd have barely enough time to plonk the plates down and hide behind the folding screen, the ottoman, or the columns, before a glittering hail of steel-blue daggers would rain down from nowhere, sticking, here and there, to the marital bed. They always seemed to be aimed straight at the beautiful Clio, but at the last minute would either vanish, or end up planted between her legs, behind her head, or on the pillow. Then they would start to melt, dripping like sparkling bouquets, the reflective surface taking in everything, exaggerating everything, giving away everything.

The Flagellant

"Three veils stuck through with needles ..." began Simone Voipoire, as she picked up a pear left in the tall grass by the girl in the white silk veil. But before she could finish her sentence she slipped in a mud puddle, plopping down in the deep, leafy grass.

The whole field, it turned out, was full of yellow pears. They were hard to see in the dying light, but some of the sunset's gleaming still made its way through the thick limbs of the forest.

Suddenly Simone began to sneeze violently, so hard her nose began to bleed. She kept on sneezing with a strange kind of pleasure, there, in the tall grass, holding a sheet of newsprint to her nose, until at last she thought she saw a golden beam of light, hard and threatening, coming at her, level with her eyes.

Hostages

for Claudine and Tom Gutt

The hostages made their way home to bed.
They were four: two men, two women.
The men paraded out front in bowler hats and moustaches, wearing robins as a boutonnieres.
Behind them, the women kept having to choke back their laughter.
The moon cast its regal light down on the little group.
Reaching the house, one of the men fumbled with his key and opened the door.
But he would go no farther.

The Woman from Alsace

My great invention, the revelation of my youth, the terrible companion of my solitude: a certain kind of girl, tall and straight, severe as a Russian beauty, scheming, cerebral, streetwise; with arms that seem to propose a solution to the problem of unexplained attraction; a certain kind of twenty-five-year-old woman; a woman who makes you think and—damn it—shuts you up. First and foremost, she shuts you up; makes you silent as a friar, so you won't miss anything about her lips, her eyes, her face: makes you want to be silent to see better. Then there's a kind of abruptly extinguished sound, her two eyes staring you down, binding you and setting you free. The kind of love she inspires is calculating: it's with you every second of every night.

A cloud of eyelashes closes in.

Riding At Night

"Perfection!" cry the horsemen.
The mountaintops shine in the moonlight.
It's a matter of getting there. It is also a matter of conquest.
It is also a matter of sand, of pebbles, of thistles all around.
There will always be time for analysis later. For the moment, only one thing matters: speed.
In every rider, from one dust cloud to the next, in the breast of each high-spirited steed, everywhere,
one urge: *speed*.
Under the sparkling sky, under the purple mesas, hard against the rolling prairie: speed.
Faster, always faster, out to the very limits of their strength: speed.
These horsemen, in their monk's cassocks.

Everyday Life

This planet spins crazily.

Soon it will have to take a sharp turn, and this means trouble, what with so many people paying to see that nothing happens.

Children are being locked away in plastic boxes, into their coffin-cribs. And women wave ragged bits of skin high in cryptic gestures. Breasts bloat with morphine, push at black silk bras—darkness holding back the light. Respectable, well-dressed gentlemen switch on all the lights in their studios, hang themselves with phone cords from their chandeliers.

Thousands of men and women arrive, eternity-eyed at the crossroads—the opened bedrooms of great cities—as if glued to one another. The makers of Universal Art.

This planet is terrible. Foreign.

The Scream

Silence.

On a night like this, down on the forest-floor, the sparking will-o-wisps might dance in the red-leafed grasses. On such a night, at the forest's edge, you watch the sprawling belt of sand, and greet the silent spectacle as hosts of little fires go creeping through the night. The moon hurls down a violence of light. This landscape only plays at sleep.

If the secret walker dares ask his question—"What is all this? What can it be?"—the forest answers with a scream.

The asker, at the forest's edge, turns fearfully to face its heart.

He finds nothing but a mass of trees, their high limbs quivering.

Delirium's Kingdom

In the distant, snow-choked valley sits the blonde, entirely naked, her hands clutching her knees tightly to her chest.

A city-suited man stands before her, his flapping scarf masking his face as he holds his arms outspread, as if to embrace her.

Little by little, first her legs, then her naked torso, and at last even her forehead and her fingers begin to blush with a glowing red. It is achingly beautiful: a color born of crackling woodfires.

For the man, now, there is nothing but the translucent nakedness of the woman, her closed eyes inventing the sky.

Snow is an aristocrat.

Sideshows of the Sky

The teacher's glare bore down into the very whites of his pupils' eyes. The students, transfixed, struggled to lower their heads. Then the teacher turned around. Then the teacher dozed off. The pupils raised their heads, quickly patting snowballs into shape.

(But if by some chance the teacher should happen to turn a suspicious eye towards them, they'll quickly change their snowballs into pen nibs, which they'll nimbly sink into the ink wells there in front of them, put there long ago for just this purpose.)

The Great Terror

In the heart of the night, who could have warned us?

Besides, don't they say that the omens of night are omens of love?

Such a tranquil breeze blew over the world, such peace breathed through the night that even the fish rested at their ease among the softly drifting sea-vines.

A few perfect, giant flowers twined their way through the rattan forest. But even then, in all the innocence of our world, a creeping doubt festered at the water's edge.

The towering palm trees felt it, and a bluish, bubbling sap bled from their trunks, spreading on the ground where it pooled, reflecting the stars burning in their remoteness.

It made no difference: all the reflections and glittering iridescences could do was make you reflect on the mysterious sources of beauty.

But what were we to make of the sudden snow that didn't fall so much as it let itself fall? The scattered flakes came down from on high, settling gently on the surface of the pond.

Bursting from the darkness of the night, that shaggy-feathered bird, its head veiled in a shroud of white silk, flapped lazily from one shore to the other, without sound.

Then a little group of horsemen, filled with fear and longing for the lost past, killed the winged thing with a crossbow.

There was no cry, nothing.

But that was the moment all life ceased.

The Lovely Little Bath

*for Helene,
and for my friend Francois Jacqmin
the Stan Getz of literature*

The Five-Cent Ultrasound

Doctor
Claude Souculare
Would declare:
Madame
You must be
A woman
And caress
Your man's
Scrotum

The Moratorium

My cousin
George
Used to say
That he adored
Taking a walk
On a warm
Summer
Day
And coming back
Worn out
At night
To end up
At the edge
Of town
Near a french fry
Stand
On fire

Darling Potatoes

My mother used to say
That
At a party
Given
By George's
Bank
George
Wanting
To show off
In front of
The bank's
Managers
Sang
In English
A language
He didn't know
At all
Nobody
Understood
A single word
Of the song
Which
Was in itself
Already
Completely
Unintelligible

Clitarabelles

for Brigitte Evers

Jacqueline
And Moniquendam
Kneel
With their pouting lips
And their drums at rest
Provoking some serious yowls
With their young breasts
While
In the ravine
Two marauders
Are seen
At twilight

Golden girls
Long legs
In the air
Of the fresh-skinned
Cooling sky

White Ducklings
Sixteen Odes in Honor of the Mystery of Israel

Stouffs sweetly puts up with the rabbi who, his throat full of brown sugar, makes a terrifying leap onto the horizontal beam—*bom*, in Swedish—landing face-to-face with Ecorce, foul-smelling player with emus, since departed.

A Cuban rabbi thinks of the woman who grew green onions, and how he Frenched her in the Bois de Boulogne.

The Latin Quarter show-offs cycle to Varennes.

If you're *really* from Prague, you long for cumin shrimp, and for the twilight to drape its ribbons over the Mustaphas who waltz at the bottom of the swimming hole.

The scrap-iron dealer pesters his proctologist.
Exhausted Ellington clutches a pint bottle.
Modern art is great when you get it.

Having abandoned her levite, the snout-tickler chooses her fish through the window on Mail Street, laughing.

The kindly earthworm makes its way across the meadow of the breasted Dianas, back to the grand hotel of Uncle Zevi, who lies dead beneath his sister.

The small children, afraid of the naked ladies, wish *shalom* to the green saws of Ra.

Pumped up by an aristocratic lass's flattery, the banker struggles against the high winds of the Fallopian tubes.

The little girl cries over the velvet, moon-embroidered belt in the *douff* sky of Marneffe.

The Caymans savor wrapped organs from the Adenauer collection.

Birehcanes loves his niece, who has come to dwell in his tent
The trumpets will come and be heard from afar
His niece often stumbles in his frock-coat
And the daffodils have bigger hard-ons for her than Birehcanes

Smah sets a balanite beside her snuffed-out cat
The hairdresser loiters and inhales the scent of tea
Young Rectine shows off her naked ass

The gardener begs his mother to let him enjoy the nuts between the pillars of Hercules of his ein-zwei-drei.

That pain-in-the-ass woman in the a bathing cap gives a cinnamon enema to the Gobi-dry rectum of the young boy who stammers "*Leyi'm plorer.*"

(for Lucy Grauman)
Al Jolson will always sing the *Kol Nidrei* for the sparrows of Paris.

These were sixteen odes in memory of the mystery of Israel.

October 1967

Uninhibited Poems

MALE AND FEMALE COUSINS, WITH TECHNICIAN

Anonymous

Note

Male and Female Cousins, with Technician is the work of an anonymous writer of the early Twentieth Century.

It features a male cousin, his female cousin and a friend of the male cousin, who happens to be a technician. Hence the title: *Male and Female Cousins, with Technician*.

Little day-to-day encounters and bits of conversation between the male cousin and the technician were noted, as they occurred, by the anonymous author.

We must also congratulate the unknown man of letters who somehow managed to classify the various pieces that make up this charming, intimate little book.

—The Editors

Urgent Poem

A watch
Or a typewriter
(Or even a calculator):
Why does the technician
Let such things lie in the office
For three weeks in a row?
It's simple:
In order to grind them up.
I put it to you bluntly.

Comfortable Poem

It's like it is with
Certain springs
(For watches
For machines
Or for parts of things,
Whatever),
There's nothing for it:
If they're too long,
It's bad;
And if they're too short,
It's bad too,
I put it to you bluntly,
If I must put it that way.

Poem Ending a Task

It's like,
The cousin says,
When the National Supply
Center
Receives an order
For linoleum:
If form 151
Isn't properly filled out,
Bang!
The order goes straight into the trash can,
I put it to you bluntly.

Poem à la Papa

There is no
Bigger pain in the ass,
The cousin says,
Than to do a favor
For my little female cousin
While the technician
Makes a discontinuous
Current
In the next room,
Because it forces
All currents,
If I must put it that way.

Poem or Not

Due to an infernal
Racket,
The technician asks
The male cousin
About the little female cousin:
What is all that
Racket.
But the male cousin says
That it's nothing,
That it's the
Refrigerator
Starting again
Just that.

PROCELEUSMATICS AND AMPHIBRAQUES

Furth-Jean Mirt

Translated from the German

Preface: Strup Stroup

We now know that the life of Furth-Jean Mirt was one of continual sacrifice and self-denial.

The poet spent most of his life in Kottbus, a small town in Hanover, with an old aunt, Madame von Salegau, née Douff.

It was the poor health of this lady, constantly surrounded by mongrels and hunting dogs, that inspired Furth-Jean to write northwest Germany's most beautiful poems.

The aunt and her nephew loved the unique countryside of the region, where potatoes, or *"Diese Parmentierspflanz,"* as Madame von Salegau would smirkingly call them, were king.

They both enjoyed long visits to the potato fields that spread out around the house as far as the eye could see; enjoyed touching the dirty-green stems; commenting on the depth of a furrow; sometimes even throwing a plant to one of the steel-gray bulldogs that accompanied them on their walks. These were extremely vigorous animals, beautiful to behold in the evening light, with the healthy firmness of their muscled hindquarters, severe and chiseled in the light of the setting sun.

Proceleusmatics and Amphibraques expresses marvelously this atmosphere of naturalistic intimacy. We would draw attention especially to "Gas Bubbles," "However a Note in the

Margin" and the famous "May They Survive Raging Tarragon."

The profound mystery hovering over the composition of the long poem "A Pedal-Pusher Said to Me" remains to be explained. It is possible that Furth-Jean wanted to record the last moments of Madame von Salegau. In any case, the poem evokes the anguish of the poet as he remembers the great rural solitudes where we can still find:

    A) the hidden croaking of the bulldogs

and

    B) the sweet spirit of his darling aunt, wrapped in a halo of *"Diese Parmentierspflanz."*

Gas Bubbles

A year and a half ago
A lady was aiming
A rolled-up piece of black paper
At the rectum of a Groenendael

Gabriel and Marcel Piqueray

May They Survive Raging Tarragon

May they survive raging tarragon
May they drink to their predecessors' auras
May the complaint about past bowel troubles
Color itself
With raging tarragon....

However a Note in The Margin

Self-referential sheets of vellum
Belonging to rare moments—
However, a note in the margin ...

Gabriel and Marcel Piqueray

If Dirty Cart-Greased to the Gaiters

If dirty, cart-greased to the gaiters,
They worked it out:
How could it fit from now on?
I make sure.

If they missed the look
Of a thing:
How could they have wagered then?
I boast.

If they wanted to be the artists
Of a stringy sweat:
What must we adore always?
I reek.

A Pedal-Pusher Said to Me

A pedal-pusher said to me
No braykaiser
No sterfput
A-stepping and a-stoumping cretin-wise
Could drive a man to madness
Just as no thousand Orphas all draped in damp peignoirs
Doing their great kochera
With the prima dona
Of Iquzegdamoda
Of Paczevast
Of Anunec
Each Orpha in an evening gown
Imploring of our pedal-pusher
To go a-step and go a-stoump all over yet again
With a thousand mops
And a thousand sterfputs imploring them
The braykaiser in me
The sterfput in me
The mop in me
The kochera in me
The Paczevast in me
The Anunec in me
The Iquzegdamoda in me
And all the stoumpers
The steppers
The mops
The evening gowns
And all the Orphas
All the pedal-pushers
The damp peignoirs

The cretins
The prima donas
Who beg
The kocheras
The Iquzegdamodas
The Anunecs
And all the Paczevasts
To step
And to stoump for the sake of love
The great flowering love
Of a thousand pedal-pushers
A-draped in damp peignoirs
Will lead no braykaiser
No sterfput
No mop
No kochera
No Paczevast
No Anunec
No Iquzegdamoda
To implore a man to madness
And that is what a-stepping and a-stoumping cretin-wise
A pedal-pusher said to me

BABY CLOTHES

Bernardin Tartar

To the Reader

Bernardin Tartar is Bulgarian, and for many years belonged to the Lovetch-Kaskeur Group, the famous pan-Bulgarian literary movement.

He is mainly known by the peasantry of the Despotodagh, the region of greenhouses, and of the remarkable Kesbazar village, of whose newborns and baby clothes he would sing, with a single, deep-breathed song.

Gabriel and Marcel Piqueray

Envoi

Bibs of Sofia, oh pretty bibs,
All boys and girls owe you the best of days!
Long live Stanimaks, long live Roumelia,
Choumen, Bourgas, Varna, Kaskei and all the counties nearby!

The Sranza de Lustuk-Obritch

Each line should be read to the rhythm of a Serbian march:
—*The Editors*

Lustuk-Obritch, in Oriental Thrace,
Rocking always your little babies pink
Lustuk-Obritch, if irksome anal fissures
Bother the bottoms of Bazouf babies pink,
You'll do well, I swear you will,
With suppositories pink.

Note

In Bernardin Tartar's writings there is, one admits, a naturalism that has its sources:

A) in the national liberation movement represented by the literary group Lovetch-Kasseur;

B) in the sincerity of the rough peasants of the Kesbazar region.

We should not forget that the poet lived for a long time with boyars, gypsies and yogurt merchants.

One finds a magnificent example of Tartar's passion for the land in his famous poem "Bulgaria, My Country," filled with tenderness, of course, but also with energy and a healthy virility.

—The Editors

Bulgaria, My Country

Under the too-heavy gold of the great church domes,
Sofia awakens. Peasants and shepherds
in their shirt-sleeves heft their tools,
Mutter to one another: "How do I look?"

Devil-bearded, they look like wild beasts,
Pike-toothed and bulge-eyed.
Their babies clutch a hundred althaea roots,
With one hundred clyster-pipes for their rattles.

On Sunday nights, families gather,
The whole town is there, bewitched by a child
Who, for want of anything better, produces turd after turd,
Each one hard as concrete.

And then, his shoes newly waxed,
Held aloft on his oil-cloth,
Facing the dumb-struck crowd, Coco lets off a fart.

HIGH EGGS

Max Merre

for Jacques Sojcher

Foreword

Max Merre is a Swiss salt-wort bicarbonate manufacturer.
Suffering from industrial poisoning, he wrote little, and in his writings we find an industrial temperament.

Calle-Grattoir

Berdellez
If
You
Mm …
Mm …
Uz …
Use me

Calle-Grattoir 2

If
You
Mm ...
Mm ...
Uz ...
Use me,
Ber ...
Ber ...
Berlaimont

Fous-La Lente

Fuck it slowly
Fuck
The bait
B ... b ... b ... b ... b ...
Berlaimont

Gabriel and Marcel Piqueray

Prose-Site

Ultra
Many
Stomp
Oh

Tout Chez (Touché)

To gallop
All alone
As an official personality
I don't understand

Gabriel and Marcel Piqueray

Uninhibited Poems

Claude de Rot en Pleine Hure

Claude de Rot en Pleine Hure is an uninhibited poet from Boston.

—The Editors

Pubis of Mite

The viscount
Recorded
A cannon shot
On an LP
Along with the "you"
Of a "thank you"
Uttered by his uncle
To a P.L.M. stage-hand.
Since the whole thing
Is repeated
For the length
Of the record
You hear:
Bang
You
Bang
You
Bang
You.
And the record,
Which lasts 15 minutes,
Ends with a bang,
But a flaw
In the recording process
Has left
(More or less
Clearly)
After the last
Bang,
The voice of

One of the technicians
Saying to a colleague:
"This is weird—
At low frequency
The ..."

The Sproks

Guy Pezasse

Preface

Guy Pezasse was a very great writer—and poet—of the 1960s. He had the ability to observe with astonishing clarity his contemporaries' actions and gestures, and to translate their daily existence into clear language.

Living in the constant company of two relatives and a friend, Guy Pezasse wrote about their daily occupations and worries with great success.

Guy Pezasse gives us the whole world, and nothing else: familiar scenes; remarkable, living situations.

The Sproks, which owes its title to Guy Pezasse's love of those fish, was written when Guy Pezasse was in his 86th year.

Guy Pezasse was to die a mere ten years later, when his lungs unaccountably stopped working.

—The Editors

Tale of an Experiment

Whenever
He gets a chance
The man
Tears a head of lettuce
Into thousands pieces
And stuffs them into a very strong
Cup of filtered coffee.
And then
He takes
What remains of the lettuce
And dumps it
Into a vat,
Dripping with coffee.

Example of an Activity

This man's uncle
Sometimes carries
An immense mattress
On his head.
And he staggers
With this mattress
From the top of the stairs
To the coal bin,
Where he lays it down
And throws himself on it
Pumping legs in the air
In excitement.

Gabriel and Marcel Piqueray

An Action Among Others

The same uncle
Who lives on the seventh floor
In the center of town
Is sometimes
In the habit of filling,
At dawn,
A large pan
With strong black coffee
And balancing it
On the window sill
With the help of his nephew;
Then sending it
Careening into the street,
Not giving a fuck
About it.

Tale of Another Action

It is this same gentleman
Who, with the help of his uncle,
Fills an immense cast-iron
Stove
With gooseberry jam.
When they've done this,
The gentleman and his uncle
Throw handfuls of jelly
At each other's faces
For fun.

An Activity Among Others

What also happens
Sometimes,
Is that the gentleman,
His uncle
And his nephew
Tear many heads of lettuce
Into thousands of pieces
Then pour strong coffee
On them,
In a vacant lot
On a slope,
With
Coal heaps
And piles of shattered windowpanes
At the bottom of the slope.
Then
They speed down the slope
On their bicycles
Without braking,
Their legs spread wide,
Feet held away from the pedals;
And then,
At the bottom of this slope,
The tires make a crackling noise
In the coal
And a farting noise
In the shattered windowpanes.
Then the gentleman,
His uncle
And his nephew

Beyond Gestures

Jump off
Their bikes
And pelt each other
With old heads of lettuce,
Very strong coffee,
Coal,
And shattered windowpanes
Until they take up shovels
While leaping
On mattresses
Filled of plaster
And pumping
Their legs in the air
In the gooseberry jelly
Of their excitement.

          Besançon 1930

Die Damen

For the women of planet Earth who, from the beginning of time, have never, even for a moment, ceased to sacrifice their bodies, hearts, minds, and lives to the simple cause of human reproduction. We say this must stop.

Private Life

for Ann West

Fickle
Women
Women
As
Deep
As
The
Sea

Gabriel and Marcel Piqueray

Young Rays

for Maria Gilissen Broodthaers

And when
We have been dead
For an unknown
Length of time
Your pond-colored
Eyes
Will,
Looking playfully
Through your
Dignified and proudly
Suffering
Tears,
See
The rainbow
Of the love
Yet unknown
To you
As
To us

Die Damen

While
A
Prophet
Rises
In
The blue sky
Along with
A multitude
Of little
Rainbow-colored
Balloons
Marcel
And
Gabriel
Their heads
Crowned with
Heaps
Of
Mauve
Lilacs
Ride
Sidesaddle
On bikes
And each is guided
By the masterful hands
Of
One
Of
A
Multitude of

Naked
Women
Into
An
Orgasm
Growing
To
The infinite
Toward the Temple of the Sun
In
Teotihuacan
Enter
Joyously
Into
The
Eyes
The
Ears
The
Lips
The
Lips
The
Mouth
The
Tongue
The
Tonsils
The
Uvula

The
Epiglottis
The
Vocal chords
The
Breasts
The navel
The rosebud
The
Palm
Of
The
Hand
The
Clitoris
The
Vagina
The
Uterus
And
The
Ass
The
Ass
D
I
S
T
R
A

U
G
H
T
The
Ass
The
Heart
Of
Die Damen

Pioneer ten moves constantly along a hyperbolic orbit, set on a trajectory for Saturn in three years, Uranus in six years, Neptune in ten years, and finally Pluto in fourteen years.

It will then enter the depths of night, and should reach the stars of the Taurus constellation in eleven million years. In case it meets intelligent life over there, it bears a gold-plated aluminum plaque on which is engraved a map of the solar system, the position of Earth in the galaxy, several scales of measurement, and finally the silhouettes of a man and a woman, the whole forming a users' manual of intelligent life on Earth.

—Renaud de la Taille

Tobacco Monument

Look at Louze

A passion for the overripe nakedness of angels, in placid, pastoral countries: this was the false premise behind her first dreams.

The day would come, she was sure, when their lily-soft songs would drape themselves across her shoulders, while she leaned passively against the rain-streaked Venetian blinds.

She really believed in this sort of thing—couldn't help it.

And it was only after dark clouds of ravens began to fill the sky that she pushed aside her innocent daydreams. She began to doubt their strength as armor. This wasn't easy for her: she'd grown to love them, lying in them as she would lie in the cool, bluish carpets of soft needles beneath the pine trees.

Now, deep in the night, the tumbling litter rustles. Pale legs move softly, waiting for strange hands that will never come.

Look at Louze and tell me, my friends, what remains of her imaginary lovers.

Her blouse drops down into a great black hole.

Laura

for Jeanine Florence and Albert Bettonville

The nostalgic, dangerous, worldly current of the canal runs strong, beneath the lonely birch-draped riverbanks in the heat of summer.

The questing gaze halts at the smoke-streaked horizon, pulling up short on its way to dark and ancient memories.

As their strands untangle, those memories sum themselves up in the plainest of images: a fashionable dress discarded by the river, where a naked Laura swims happily, eyes fixed on the paleness of the sky. It was the festival season.

Flowing Water

At twilight, the rain spurs the taut flank of the water.

Ardente lounges in the pond's shallows, eyes turned to the sky, elbows leaning on the dark and mossy bank.

Nearby, the sheen of her sand-yellow handbag, all chrome and leather, brings to mind old bison, steam engines, dumbbells lifted by virile men in large, empty rooms.

Ardente rummages through it, pulls out some cyclamen lipstick, applies it carefully to her parted lips, then blots them over and over.

She rises from the water and makes her way into a grove of trees, from which then comes a sudden laughter, a child's laughter, a jerky laughter that grows louder and louder, then stops abruptly.

Night falls with the rain.

The leather bag still shines in the grass, its soggy strap sagging there.

The Hungarian

I've got to fill my glass. Absolutely.

Over by the carafe, the radio warms up, crackling with static.

The lodger from the next room says it's a power surge, that the air is too muggy. Where does he get off talking like that around me? What's his logic here?

The landlady comes in crying, says that war has been declared.

So it's off to join our regiments.

As I head out, I notice that my glass, has, conveniently, been filled.

Professionals

Having scaled the wall, they leapt over the bristling shards of broken glass, hoping to land softly in the slop-pile left over from last year's meager scrapings.

As they fell endlessly, they came to the conclusion that they must have picked the wrong wall. Growing used to the void, they started to think of other things.

Gabriel and Marcel Piqueray

Light

for Boris, for my Jewish sisters, and for my Jewish brothers

Mute as a Carp
the film by Boris Lehman,
moves me deeply.

Bathtub (murder)
Generic (animation)
Pond (fishing)
Fishmarket (large spaces)
Kitchen (preparation—chanting in the synagogue)
Prayer at the edge of the canal
Lighting of the candles (grandmother)
Meal (prayer—slower pacing)

The Pond
The Night

Sin
Purity
Veiled
Unveiled

Teach
Oh Jew!
Yes, the omnipresence
Of white

Tablecloth
Refrigerator
Shallow pan
Car trunk

Yes, night
Yes, murder

Yes, the ancestors
Yes, the cantor
Yes, the blood
In the tub
Yes, the glass of red wine
Spilled
On the white tablecloth

Yes, we are all of us,
Women
And
Men,
Carp

Sometimes one of them
Succeeds
For a while
In escaping
The nets
Of Death

No to the Shoah
No to sacrifice
This shadow of reality
Calls out with a psalm of David

Here is
The meeting
The plenitude
The fervor
The blessing

The Table
Of the Feast
Of "eating together"

Only
Innocence
Remains
You understand
Innocence

The good

Unpublished Writings

The Lover

for Yih-Ching
Luc Rémy
and Dexter Gordon

His long solitude sharpens his attention to the frolic of seagulls.

They fight noisily for the smallest crumbs and the tiniest crusts of bread.

Yet they remain, always, together.

Far past his last point of reference, a bystander, he gapes in awe at the roiling waves of the virgin sea, settles himself on a park bench, begins to dream.

Soon the strolling passers-by, finding the lover, will feel the cold shock of the truth,
his death.

—Gabriel Piqueray
(last poem, September 1991)

Gabriel and Marcel Piqueray

Heart Phosphor

for Eliane, and Jean-Michel Pochet

Birds
Detergents
Fatigues
Lost time
Medicines to cure the uneasiness of great
Orchestras

The tiny little girl
Is
Dead

She
Did
Not
Choose
The
Authoritative
Team
Of an
Unarmed
German
Pontius
Peter
Shabbat

Tango
Of
The ecologists
The fountain-maker

Prefers
Wheat

Land

Thamar

High sea

Abysses
Abysses
Abysses

Money

Concrete
Concrete
Concrete
Concrete

Things
Things
Things
Things

Blood

In the summer, in the evening, under a greengage sky, ancient wire ties the periwinkles to the edge of the night: catgut for the memory of love.

Gabriel and Marcel Piqueray

The Sealed Mountain

for Yv.
Karann
Elisabeth
Marc Moulin
Philippe Dewolf
and for Philip Catherine

How slow it is! Glorious, endless work, no matter how high you climb.

The invisible Man.
A flare goes off whistling, falls back slowly, and snuffs out next to four dead sheep.

A woman, smelling of fresh bread and of warm water, forty years old, a geologist, stoops, examining a stone.

You can just make out the love-words on her lips.
Another corpse.

Blue sky, biting-sharp.
Lone white cloud, scudding away.

Uncertainty in Love

for Karann
Françoise
Luc
Fabienne
Isabelle
Yvan
Nathalie
Erik
for Benny Carter
and for Carla Bley

There is no one on whole wide beach, except for Guy, who is waiting for Françoise.

The cut stems lie on the sand, damp and cool on the palms of your hands.

The dune, piled precariously and covered with yellow wildflowers, seems to slide down toward the waterline.

Beside a beach house, a barrel drum, lidless and three-quarters full of drifting sand, smells of tar.

Françoise doesn't seem to be coming.

Guy, dreaming, sights a cormorant near the shore, alone on its almost sunken rock, poised to dive into the water.

C'est la vie.

Great white clouds, blinding bright, bar the wide horizon.

Gabriel and Marcel Piqueray

For My Fiancée
for Annie

The Charity of Saint Christopher
Comes to meet you
My beautiful English bird
Deep sea in the bright hours of the night
The palms of your hands quench the thirst of the leprous women
I see you adorned like Diane de Poitiers
Wearing a hemp belt
And rough leather shoes
I see you fleeing the instruments of torture
Making the sign of the cross at the church door
Taking the place of the sky

You are more lake than the lakes
You are more doe than the does
You are more beautiful than yourself

The fullness of luxury
Lips to lips body to body
The bouquet of the eyes as blonde as night

You are a tidal wave
With arms of the sea
With breasts of dunes
With sex of avalanche
With legs of velvet
With a belfry heart

Love is raging

—Marcel Piqueray, 1943

Gudrun

for Michele Noiret
for Anna-Angelica dos Santos
Ines Amarante
and Ivone do Carmo Lauria
for Y. B.
for the Ransart sisters
for Miles Davis

Wistaria

The lightning of the unforgettably great flirts: impossible for it to be random

Distant chrysanthemums of love, all of them buried despite the darkness of the night

The sun, high in midsummer, throws light on the pale gravel at the edge of the forest

You

Your low-heeled shoes

Like fairy tales told by friends: your delicate, pale lipstick, the color of sifted cinnamon

Horizon   Platinum   Ocean

About the Authors

GABRIEL AND MARCEL PIQUERAY were identical twins, born in Brussels in 1920. Surrealists, they associated with key figures of the movement, including André Breton and René Magritte (with whom they held regular "surrealist working meetings" for many years), as well as with the musician Chet Baker and the composer Francis Poulenc. In 1957 they became joint editors of the influential avant-garde journal *Phantomas*, whose contributors included Samuel Beckett, Roland Barthes, René Magritte, Kurt Schwitters, and Jorge Luis Borges, among many others. They published a dozen books together, always listing "Gabriel and Marcel Piqueray" as authors—the Piqueray brothers did not believe in individual authorship. Gabriel died in 1992 and Marcel five years later.

ROBERT ARCHAMBEAU is a novelist, poet, and critic. His books include the novel *Alice B. Toklas is Missing*, the poetry collections *Home and Variations* and *The Kafka Sutra*, the essay collections *The Poet Resigns* and *Inventions of a Barbarous Age*, and the critical studies *Laureates and Heretics* and *Poetry and Uselessness from Coleridge to Ashbery*.

JEAN-LUC GARNEAU is a linguist whose books include *Semantic Divergence in Anglo-French Cognates* and the collection of stories and poems *La rivière des morts*.

www.ingramcontent.com/pod-product-compliance
Lightning Source LLC
Chambersburg PA
CBHW020334170426
43200CB00006B/387

Praise for *Beyond Gestures*

Being Belgian and writing in French, the Piqueray twins were influenced by Surrealism, as seen in the paintings of René Magritte and Paul Delvaux, images of dreamlike disjunction that, according to Surrealism's founder, Andre Breton, represented the Absolute. The real truth was to be found in the uncanny and its twin sister, eroticism. The Piqueray brothers were not, however, programmatic, as Breton proved to be. In their poem, "Light," dedicated to their Jewish sisters and brothers, we are touched by history: "Yes, the ancestors / Yes, the cantor / Yes, the blood / In the tub / Yes, the glass of red wine / Spilled / on the white tablecloth." This is a wonderful collection, and it arrives just at the right time. —Paul Hoover

Beyond Gestures breathes vitality into the compact narratives crafted by the Franco-Belgian twins, Gabriel and Marcel Piqueray, who occupied a central role in the development of European surrealism. Their translators, Robert Archambeau and Jean-Luc Garneau skillfully capture the recurrent sense in these works of a beguiling, quirky, sometimes humorous or satirical—and occasionally weird—admixture of storytelling, quotidian observation, idiosyncratic commentary and childlike evocation. These translations convey a compelling sense of the imaginative lives of two writers who identified with one other so closely that they claimed joint authorship for everything they wrote. This volume holds countless delights.
—Cassandra Atherton

Two poets in Brussels, part of the surrealist mileau that gave rise to Cobra, the Situationists, Phases ... they continued a hidden Surrealist activity with their friends during the war and occupation and published poetry with the great printmaker Pierre Alechinsky. Surrealism speaks here: dreams and everyday life, chance and madness, automatism and experiment. —Penelope Rosemont